WOODLAND PUBLIC LIBRARY

3 1652 00148 8049

T1-AYR-941

The CHANGING FACE *of* AMERICAN SOCIETY

1945–2000

J
973.92
COL
2002

"The CHANGING FACE *of* AMERICAN SOCIETY

1945–2000

Christopher Collier
James Lincoln Collier

BENCHMARK BOOKS

MARSHALL CAVENDISH
NEW YORK

ACKNOWLEDGMENT: The authors wish to thank Harvard Sitkoff for his careful reading of the text of this volume of The Drama of American History and his thoughtful and useful comments. The work has been much improved by Professor Sitkoff's notes. The authors are deeply in his debt, but, of course, assume full responsibility for the substance of the work, including any errors that may appear.

Photo research by James Lincoln Collier.
COVER PHOTO: Corbis/Bettman
PICTURE CREDITS: *New York Public Library*: 11, 17, 27; *Corbis/Bettman*: 13,15, 16, 18, 21, 24 (top & bottom), 31, 32, 33, 37, 39, 41 (top & bottom), 42, 43, 47, 48, 49, 51, 53, 55 (top & bottom), 59 (top and bottom), 65, 66, 67, 68, 71, 75, 77; *Author's private collection*: 57, 74, 79, 80, 82.

Benchmark Books
Marshall Cavendish Corporation
99 White Plains Road
Tarrytown, New York 10591-9001

©2002 Christopher Collier and James Lincoln Collier

All rights reserved. No part of this book may be reproduced or utilized in any form or by any means electronic or mechanical, including photocopying, recording, or by any information storage and retrieval system, without permission from the copyright holders.

Library of Congress Cataloging-in-Publication Data

Collier, Christopher, 1930–
     The changing face of America, 1945–2000 / by Christopher Collier and
James Lincoln Collier.
          p. cm. – (Drama of American history)
     Includes bibliographical references (p.) and index.
     ISBN 0-7614-1319-7
     1. United States—History—1945—Juvenile literature. 2. United States—Social conditions—
1945—Juvenile literature. 3. United States—Social life and customs—20th century—Juvenile literature. [1. United States—History—1945– 2. United States—Social conditions—1945– 3. United
States—Social life and customs—20th century.]
          I. Collier, James Lincoln, 1928–

E741 .C52 2001
973.92—dc21   2001025963

Series designed by Sylvia Frezzolini Severance

Printed in Italy

1 3 5 6 4 2

CONTENTS

PREFACE

Over many years of both teaching and writing for students at all levels, from grammar school to graduate school, it has been borne in on us that many, if not most, American history textbooks suffer from trying to include everything of any moment in the history of the nation. Students become lost in a swamp of factual information, and as a consequence lose track of how those facts fit together and why they are significant and relevant to the world today.

In this series, our effort has been to strip the vast amount of available detail down to a central core. Our aim is to draw in bold strokes, providing enough information, but no more than is necessary, to bring out the basic themes of the American story, and what they mean to us now. We believe that it is surely more important for students to grasp the underlying concepts and ideas that emerge from the movement of history, than to memorize an array of facts and figures.

The difference between this series and many standard texts lies in what has been left out. We are convinced that students will better remember the important themes if they are not buried under a heap of names, dates, and places.

In this sense, our primary goal is what might be called citizenship education. We think it is critically important for America as a nation and Americans as individuals to understand the origins and workings of the public institutions that are central to American society. We have asked ourselves again and again what is most important for citizens of our democracy to know so they can most effectively make the system work for them and the nation. For this reason, we have focused on political and institutional history, leaving social and cultural history less well developed.

This series is divided into volumes that move chronologically through the American story. Each is built around a single topic, such as the Pilgrims, the Constitutional Convention, or immigration. Each volume has been written so that it can stand alone, for students who wish to research a given topic. As a consequence, in many cases material from previous volumes is repeated, usually in abbreviated form, to set the topic in its historical context. That is to say, students of the Constitutional Convention must be given some idea of relations with England, and why the Revolution was fought, even though the material was covered in detail in a previous volume. Readers should find that each volume tells an entire story that can be read with or without reference to other volumes.

Despite our belief that it is of the first importance to outline sharply basic concepts and generalizations, we have not neglected the great dramas of American history. The stories that will hold the attention of students are here, and we believe they will help the concepts they illustrate to stick in their minds. We think, for example, that knowing of Abraham Baldwin's brave and dramatic decision to vote with the small states at the Constitutional Convention will bring alive the Connecticut Compromise, out of which grew the American Senate.

Each of these volumes has been read by esteemed specialists in its particular topic; we have benefited from their comments.

CHAPTER I

Sudden Wealth

When we hear the word "history," we usually think of generals, bloody battles, hard-fought presidential elections, empires rising and falling. And it is certainly true that the outcomes of battles and elections can have major effects on people, sometimes wonderful, sometimes dreadful.

But as actually experienced by people, history is more often about subtler, harder to define changes that affect how we live our daily lives. Such things as new inventions, the coming and going of financially good and bad times, or the development of new ways of doing business may have more of an impact on human life than a war or a presidential election. Just think how important a simple thing like the development of the credit card, or the invention of frozen food, has been in American life.

This book is about that sort of history—which is usually called *social history*—during the years from the end of World War II to the end of the twentieth century. It is about dramatic changes to American life brought about by two phenomena. One was the astonishing prosperity which swept America beginning at the war's end and continued into the twenty-first century, with, of course, some temporary setbacks. The second is an equally astonishing change in attitudes toward behavior that began to crop up in the 1950s, grew explosively in the late 1960s, and took over in the 1970s. We must understand that both the kind of wealth we take for granted today and the feelings and beliefs we have about money, sex, drugs, and much else would have astonished most Americans had they been able to look forward from 1945 to the new world coming. (The political history of the period is described in two previous volumes in this series, called *The United States in the Cold War, 1945–1991* and *The Middle Road: American Politics, 1945–2000*.)

When World War II ended in 1945 the largest number of Americans lived in cities. Suburbs had started to develop early in the century, but they remained small and housed mostly the well-to-do, who commuted to work in the central cities by train or even trolley cars. Forty percent of American families did not own a car, and among ordinary working people it was more than half. The two-car family was a rarity. There were no superhighways, and the few "parkways" in use ran fewer than fifty miles and had at the most two lanes in each direction.

Only a half dozen or so shopping malls existed—there were none, for example, in the New York City area. Downtown department stores, like Marshall Field's in Chicago and Hudson's in Detroit, were in their glory days; people shopped there, or in smaller clothing, jewelry, and five-and-ten-cent stores in their neighborhoods, traveling by bus, subway, or on foot.

And they bought far less: Much of what we find in American homes today was owned only by the wealthy, or did not exist at all. In 1945 commercial television, as a practical matter, did not exist. Only well-to-do families had more than one radio; most had one that sat in the living room and was shared by all. Many families did not have a record player; the records themselves were the old 78s that played for three minutes and shattered when dropped. There were no tape cassettes or CD players.

Some housewives had rudimentary washing machines, but many still washed the family's clothes by hand. There were no dryers; clothes were

When World War II ended in 1945 not only were there hardly any shopping malls, but self-service supermarkets were just being established. People bought most of their food at the corner grocery store, where a clerk helped each customer to get what she needed. This Stop & Shop, started in 1946 right after the war, is an early example of a supermarket.

hung on lines, or in bad weather strung around the house on folding racks or over chairs. Frozen food was only beginning to come in. Vegetables were either canned, or bought fresh to be washed, peeled, chopped, and sliced by hand. Except among the wealthy, socks with holes in them were not thrown away, but were darned; worn clothes were patched, and younger children were expected to wear hand-me-downs from their older brothers and sisters.

Young people had very little money of their own. A typical allowance for a twelve-year-old—for those who got any at all—might be a dime or a quarter a week. (An ice-cream cone or a Coke cost a nickel.) A school-child might earn small amounts of money, fifteen cents or twenty-five cents an hour, baby-sitting or selling newspapers. Older boys might earn a little more delivering groceries or mowing lawns. A lot of young people found it necessary to save their money for things their families could not afford to buy them, like baseball gloves and roller skates. In many working families young people were expected to contribute part or all of their earnings to the family.

Most wives worked at home. Among the middle class hardly any mothers of small children had jobs; in the blue-collar classes more women worked, but even here the majority worked at home. (*Blue-collar* is a term for hourly-wage workers in factories and such, as contrasted to *white-collar* workers in offices, who are usually salaried.) Among other things, a wife and mother had enough to do at home, minding small children, washing, cooking, and cleaning, to keep her busy all day long.

As we shall see later in this volume, there were many reasons that large numbers of women entered the workforce in the second half of the twentieth century. But perhaps most significant were the changing ideas of the times—attitudes toward right and wrong, how many *things* a family needed in order to live a middle-class life, what was the proper role of women. Most people then—so soon after the Great Depression of the 1930s—felt it was wrong to spend money unnecessarily; the idea was to be prudent and save for something important or for a "rainy day." Traditionally, too, Americans felt that it was more important to work hard than to enjoy themselves. The aim of life was not just to accumulate material goods and have a good time but to be responsible, work hard, and get ahead.

Drugs did exist, but most ordinary people were horrified by the very idea of using them, and many had only a vague idea of what they were. Sex outside of marriage was hardly uncommon—it never has been—but most people believed that a girl who had sex before she was married had done something quite wrong. A double standard applied almost everywhere, so men were not condemned for similar conduct. A woman who had a baby without being married would be looked down on, even shunned, by others. Divorce was hardly unusual, either, but by far the

Before the war a radio of this kind sat in middle-class homes. The family would gather around it to listen to favorite shows. People of modest means would have small radios. Many families could not afford a radio at all and would visit friends to listen to special shows.

majority of married people stayed married for their lifetimes. Magazines like *Playboy* could not be openly sold. Cursing was forbidden on radio and in the movies; when the word "damn" was used in the movie *Gone With the Wind* in 1939, it created a sensation. Sex could not be described in novels or shown on screens. In sum, most Americans believed that the aim of life was not merely to seek pleasure or express themselves but to be responsible and work hard—from which they felt great personal satisfaction.

America in 2000 was a very different place. Many people believe that they should have what they want when they want it, and carry high amounts of debt in order to do so. The use of drugs was widespread; sex outside marriage, commonplace. Perhaps most significantly, in 1945 the vast majority of Americans lived in families consisting of working fathers, stay-at-home mothers, and children. By 2000, only 7 percent did. This is a major change of lifestyle. How did it come about?

During the 1930s the United States (and much of the world) suffered from the worst economic depression in its history. At times 25 percent of workers were unemployed; children in poverty-stricken regions, like the Appalachian Mountain region, went without shoes and many families often went to bed hungry at night. Nothing the government or anybody else could do helped.

In 1933 the Japanese invaded China, and in 1939 the Germans invaded Poland; World War II began. In 1941 the Japanese bombed the American naval base in Hawaii, and the United States was drawn into the war. The government began to buy immense quantities of military supplies, borrowing a lot of money to help pay for them. There were jobs for everybody; prosperity suddenly returned.

With American factories busy turning out tanks, bullets, and military uniforms, there were no new cars, stoves, bicycles, or much else coming into the stores. Until 1945, when factories could convert back to making peacetime goods, Americans did without, and saved up a lot of money. When goods finally became available, they were snapped up. Many had feared that the end of the war might bring back the Depression, but with people buying so much with the money they had saved during the war, the economy remained strong. Then, in 1950, the United States got into the Korean War. Once again there was a great demand for military supplies as well as civilian goods, and the economy grew even stronger.

Helping to keep it that way was a federal program of aid for returning soldiers and sailors called the GI Bill of Rights. (GI stood for *government issue*; soldiers were often called GIs.) One thing this program did was to provide money for school and college tuitions. Veterans from blue-collar families, who in earlier times might never have considered going to college or even finishing high school, entered college and went on to have careers as doctors, lawyers, business executives. In the end 2 million veterans went to college on the GI Bill. During the 1950s millions of fathers and mothers with callused hands proudly watched their children graduate from famous universities. The effect on prosperity of this large increase in college graduates was indirect, but it was real, for it moved millions of

Soldiers, like these paratroopers, benefited from the GI Bill, which helped to pay their college expenses and gave them inexpensive loans that allowed them to buy houses, cars, and other important things, thus boosting the American economy after the war.

people into more productive, better-paying white-collar jobs.

The GI Bill also offered low-cost loans for the purchase of houses. Eager builders began throwing up inexpensive housing "developments" on former potato fields and pastures, using mass-production techniques and standard plans that gave the houses a basically similar look. The most famous of these mass producers of houses was William Levitt. He worked out a system of using prefabricated parts and then assembling the houses on foundations built for the purpose. His famous Levittown on Long Island, outside New York City, eventually comprised over 17,000 homes, which sold in 1946 for $7,900, with no down payment because under the GI Bill the U.S. Government would pay the mortgage if the buyer defaulted.

Previously, the idea of owning a home, much less a new one, had seemed an impossible dream to millions of Americans, especially those

The famous Levittown on Long Island as it appeared in 1954. At first the town had strict rules about what color owners could paint their houses or the kinds of bushes they could plant. There were many complaints about its uniformity. However, the system of construction allowed houses to be built quickly and cheaply.

blue-collar families. All of a sudden, young wives and husbands who had grown up in big-city cold-water apartments, sharing their bedrooms with two or three of their brothers or sisters, discovered that they could buy their own homes. The houses in Levittown and similar places sold as fast as they could be built. Very quickly, new suburbs began to spread around America's cities. In 1944 about 100,000 houses were built in all of the United States; in 1950 it was over a million. By 1960 one-third of Americans lived in the suburbs.

These new houses needed new refrigerators, stoves, beds, carpets, and a great deal else. Furthermore, these new suburbs were farther out from the central cities than the older suburbs. The new suburbanites needed cars to get to work, to get to the railroad station, to shop, to ferry kids around. Automobile sales jumped. So did traffic problems. In 1950, we should realize, making a trip by car for any distance meant driving right through the downtown areas of towns and cities along the way. President Eisenhower, who took office in 1953, saw the need for a vast new federal highway system, in part for military use in case of an emergency, but also to help makers of cars, gasoline, cement, and other materials increase their businesses. Of course building better roads was popular with automobile-owning voters, too. Over the next decades the federal government spent billions of dollars building the system of interstate highways we now take for granted. We see, then, that prosperity, which

In 1950 this Ford advertisement advanced the amazing idea that a family could own more than one car—at a time when many families didn't own a car at all. Today the two-car family is common-place, and many families have three or even more.

In 1951 the Census Bureau proclaimed the family of Robert Rehm the "average" American family, with a stay-at-home wife, a working husband, two children, and a dog. Mr. Rehm earned about $3,000 a year, owned a radio, a refrigerator, and a telephone. The two children in this picture, Chris and Jeff Rehm, could be grandparents today.

probably would have come in the wake of wartime spending, was helped along by continued government spending.

On top of everything, the birthrate soared. During the Depression many young people had been too poor to start families; in wartime millions of young men were away in the army. With the return of the servicemen, people who had put off marriage started families. These women, with their husbands enjoying new jobs with high wages, had the money to move out of cramped apartments into the new suburban houses; there they had the space to have larger families. The number of families with three children tripled; those with four grew four times. Between 1950 and 1960 America's population jumped from 150 million to 179 million. The "baby boom" of 1946 to 1964 helped to keep prosperity rolling: More children meant a greater demand for clothes, blankets, bicycles, school buildings.

There was one more factor. Before the Depression, which began in 1930, the labor unions of blue-collar workers, despite much struggle and many strikes, had not been able to improve conditions for workers much. Wages stayed low; indeed, many workers and their families lived on the edge of poverty all their lives. During the Depression President Franklin Roosevelt's New Deal pushed through laws to aid the unions in their struggle against the industrial managers. During the war the demand for labor forced wages up. After the war, unions found themselves in a much stronger position and were able to demand wage increases to go along with the new prosperity. This insured that workers would have money in their pockets to buy the things they were making. (Roosevelt's programs are described in the volume in this series called *Progressivism, the Depression, and the New Deal*.)

It will be clear that an upward spiral was running: The great demand for goods kept the factories humming, providing plenty of jobs at good wages. Critically important, however, were the vast sums the government was spending for the highway program, the GI Bill, and especially the military: By 1950 the United States was engaged in the Cold War against the Soviet Union, which forced both sides to keep escalating their weapons systems to match the other. Taken altogether between 1945 and 1960, the *gross national product*, or GNP (the total value of all goods and services produced), went from $200 billion to $500 billion. Between 1956 and 1970 the GNP doubled. The United States, with 6 percent of the world's population, was producing *two-thirds* of the world's manufactured goods and consuming a third of them.

The net effect was to very greatly expand the middle class. Previously, white-collar workers in offices made substantially larger wages than blue-collar workers on the factory floor, and lived better sorts of lives, with different dreams and aspirations. With the new prosperity, the gap began to close. Now many blue-collar workers could enjoy things that in the past only white-collar workers possessed, like houses, cars, college educations for their children. As a result, the definition of "middle class" changed: Why shouldn't a family that owned a car, a house, and a television set consider itself middle class, even if the father worked with his hands?

The American economy with the help of large government expenditures was thus constantly rising. A more prosperous people were buying more things, producing substantial profits that could be invested to make even more things. But there were other factors. For one, much of the world remained poor. American industry was able to buy from abroad a host of raw materials at low prices. Cheap oil was critically important as the demand for it in the United States outran the American supply, but there were many other items, including rubber, tin, and sugar, that were scarce in the United States or could be bought cheaper elsewhere.

For another, Americans have long had a tradition of innovation and experimentation. Rather than continue to do things in the same way year after year, as many people in more traditional cultures did, American industrialists were always looking for cheaper, better, and faster ways of doing things. Productivity, with each worker producing more per hour, rose steadily.

Through the twentieth century American prosperity continued to surge ahead. Children who had struggled in the 1930s to save enough money for a football or a fishing rod, in the 1960s were giving their own children heaps of athletic equipment more advanced than what professional athletes had used twenty years earlier. By the 1990s those children, now grown up, were buying for their own children things that in the 1960s could only have been bought by the rich—like their own color television sets—or had not existed at all, such as video games.

True, there have been slowdowns, even steps backward. The 1970s were hard at times, relatively speaking. But the drive has been ever upward. Between 1950 and 2000 the per capita (per person) gross national product more than tripled. That is to say, as hard as it is to believe, in the year 2000 the average American could have *three times* as much in goods and services as he or she could have had in 1950—three times as many pairs of shoes, three times as many fast-food meals, three times as many radios and everything else. In half a century the United States had become enormously wealthy.

The effects were felt by other nations. By the 1970s some of them were catching up, and by the 1990s a few, particularly Japan and the western European nations, were not far behind. However, most of the rest of the world was living on a fraction of what Americans had. The

Before the Depression, governments usually sided with the corporations against the strikers. In the famous Baltimore & Ohio Railroad strike, in 1877, troops actually fired on the strikers.

Communist nations, during the 1970s and 1980s especially, suffered by comparison. Although they were industrialized, for a variety of reasons they simply could not produce anything like the goods flowing out of American factories. Leaders of countries like the Soviet Union and China tried to keep their people from learning about America's prosperity, but Chinese and Russian people often managed to see American magazines, movies, and television. They learned how much better off Americans were. Their dissatisfaction was one major reason why communism collapsed in the Soviet Union, and why at the turn of the twentieth century Chinese leaders were attempting to bring in at least some elements of the free-enterprise system.

CHAPTER II

A Better Deal for African-Americans

Before the Civil War (1861–1865) most blacks lived in the South, almost all as slaves. There were small numbers of free blacks in the North, and an even smaller number in the South. The Civil War ended slavery, and for ten years or so thereafter, during a period called Reconstruction, it appeared that the freedmen, under the protection of federal troops stationed in the South, might begin to enjoy the *civil rights* whites had—the right to vote, equal treatment from state governments, the right to own real estate, to start businesses, to go to school.

But when federal troops were withdrawn in 1877, Reconstruction ended, and white southerners began, through what were called "Jim Crow" laws, to push African-Americans back into a condition that was not much better than slavery. Blacks were prevented from voting through state laws and when the laws failed, through trickery and intimidation. They were given only inferior schools. They found it difficult to get good jobs, which were always reserved for whites, and ended up scraping out bare livings, eating the poorest food, wearing ragged clothing. By law they were forced to use separate theaters, restaurants, public drinking fountains, and toilets. Far worse, blacks were sometimes lynched without

In the South, Jim Crow laws required blacks and whites to use different drinking fountains.

FOR COLORED ONLY

Waiting rooms were also seg-regated, as in this Trailways bus terminal in Jackson, Mississippi. Some of the worst violence of the Civil Rights move-ment came during the effort to inte-grate waiting rooms and other trans-portation facilities.

COLORED WAITING ROOM
INTRASTATE PASSENGERS

trial for crimes, or even when they had committed no crime. By the 1890s there were sometimes as many as a hundred lynchings a year. In that era no white person was ever convicted of these murders.

Conditions in the North were considerably better. Lynching was rare, blacks could attend schools and ride on trains and buses along with whites, and use the same drinking fountains. But still, they were usually able to get only the lowest-paying jobs, and as a result most lived on the edge of poverty in run-down neighborhoods, although there were always a few blacks in the North who managed to rise in business and the professions.

Nobody has ever convincingly explained why racial prejudice exists, though hundreds of scholars have tried to. However, it seems to exist everywhere in some version: People of most groups tend to look down on those from other groups, whatever their race or nationality. American racial prejudice against African-Americans is hardly unique. And like racial prejudice elsewhere, it has proved very difficult to overcome. In the early days it seemed to most whites, even those opposed to slavery, that blacks were basically inferior to whites—not as clever, talented, or capable of living in civilized ways. In fact, African-Americans were caught in a trap: Given the worst educations—or none, growing up in poverty and slum conditions, and eating poor diets, black children started life at a severe disadvantage compared to white children.

Thus matters stood when World War II began. Although there had always been some blacks in the military, for the most part they worked at menial tasks, and had difficulty rising through the ranks. But with the entry of America into World War II in 1941, it was clear that the nation must use all the manpower available. Prejudice was hard to overcome: The military did not quickly bring African-Americans into combat. But in time, half a million blacks served overseas, many of them fighting, usually in their own units under white officers.

The wartime manpower shortage also made it possible for blacks to get jobs in war plants. However, they were hired mainly as sweepers, janitors, and loaders, the most low-paying sorts of jobs. As the war plants went into high speed in 1940, blacks saw white workers earning sizable wage packets, while they got only rock-bottom pay. In January 1941 a celebrated African-American leader, A. Philip Randolph, head of the Brotherhood of Sleeping Car Porters (working as a porter was traditionally a black job), put forth a plan to have as many as a hundred thousand blacks march on Washington to demand a fair share of jobs in the defense industry. President Roosevelt tried to persuade him to call it off. Though Roosevelt at heart wanted to improve conditions for blacks, he did not want to antagonize southern congressmen, whose votes he needed for his programs. He knew a march on Washington was sure to arouse the ire of southerners. But Randolph was determined to go through with the march, and in the end Roosevelt issued an executive order that said, "There shall be no discrimination in the employment of workers in defense industries because of race, creed, color, or national origin . . . ." Congress then established a Fair Employment Practice Committee to see that blacks were not kept out of the good jobs.

Although blacks began to get a fairer share of good jobs, these actions by no means ended their problems. Job openings in war plants had drawn tens of thousands of southern blacks to northern cities. Many whites disliked seeing blacks move into their neighborhoods, using their parks and beaches. Tensions ran high and at times broke into violence. There were several race riots. The worst of these occurred in Detroit in June 1943, when several hundred blacks and whites fought in the city streets. Roosevelt finally called in troops, but twenty-five blacks and nine whites were dead. Similar, if smaller, riots took place in other cities.

With the war's end, many African-Americans came out of the military service determined to fight racism at home. They had risked their lives for democracy, why should they be discriminated against at home? Franklin Roosevelt died in the spring of 1945. He was succeeded by his vice president, Harry S. Truman. In 1946 Truman appointed a committee to see what could be done about blacks' civil rights, and asked Congress to act. Congress had powerful southerners in many key committees, and refused to enact Truman's program. However, as commander in chief of the military, Truman ordered the services to integrate. During the Korean War, which began in June 1950, more and more units were integrated; by August 1951, 30 percent of the units in the army were racially mixed.

Still, it was only beginning to be possible for African-Americans to

During the Korean War fighting units increasingly became racially mixed. Happy soldiers hear on the radio that a peace treaty has been agreed to.

register at good hotels, or get seats in many restaurants. Blacks were barred from playing in the major leagues (although they had their own leagues) until 1947, when Jackie Robinson broke baseball's color barrier as a first baseman with the Brooklyn Dodgers. In the South all children by law went to racially segregated schools.

There had always been many whites who were sympathetic to the problems of blacks. There were not enough of them, however, and by 1950 many African-Americans were convinced that they would have to fight their own battles. Thus there began, in the years after World War II, a long drive by blacks to improve conditions for themselves. This drive is known as the civil rights movement. Some whites did help, joining black organizations and helping to register black voters in the South. But the leadership, and most of the push, came from African-Americans.

America had long adhered to the rule, laid down by the Supreme Court in 1896 in *Plessy* v. *Ferguson*, of "separate but equal"—that is, segregation was acceptable under the Constitution, provided that blacks had waiting rooms, buses, public toilets, and especially schools that were as good as the white ones. In reality, however, black schools were vastly inferior: Southern states spent much less, sometimes as little as 10 percent, educating each black child as each white one. White teachers' salaries were 30 to 100 percent higher than those of black teachers.

African-Americans had long believed that education was a key to black improvement: Badly educated blacks had trouble competing for jobs with better-schooled whites. In 1950 the leaders of the then most important black organization, the National Association for the Advancement of Colored People (NAACP), decided to go to court to challenge the forced racial segregation of schools. Heading the battle was a black lawyer, Thurgood Marshall, who would later be appointed to the Supreme Court.

In fact, Marshall had already been involved in lawsuits against segregated education. As far back as the 1930s, in the so-called *Gaines* case, he persuaded the Supreme Court to rule that a tax-supported state law school could not deny admission to blacks—who, after all, also paid state taxes. Marshall knew that there would be less resistance by white southerners to breaking down walls in higher education than there would be to integrating elementary and high schools. Marshall and his group then brought a number of cases against segregation in southern law and graduate schools. Part of their scheme was to force southern states to bring their schools for blacks up to the level of those for whites. The expense for the states would be enormous, and they might well choose to integrate their schools, which would be a lot cheaper. But Marshall had another idea, which was that the very fact of segregation was of itself unconstitutional and unequal. In these cases Marshall and his group had some victories and some defeats, but gradually the courts began to accept the idea that segregation was "inherently unequal," because it implied that blacks were inferior to whites. Giving African-American school children the feeling that they were inferior would "retard their educational and mental development."

All of this led up to one of the most famous cases in Supreme Court history, known as *Brown* v. *Board of Education*. First, Marshall sued school systems in several cities—not all southern—over segregated schools. He got distinguished psychologists to testify that being kept out of white schools did, indeed, give black children a sense of inferiority. They expected to lose in the lower courts, even in northern states like Kansas, and did. Marshall now took the Kansas case to the Supreme Court. After much argument, and several hearings, on May 17, 1954, the Supreme Court handed down its famous ruling: Segregation created "a feeling of inferiority in black children which might gravely damage them," thus official segregation of public schools violated the U.S. Constitution because it deprived people of the "equal protection of the law" guaranteed by the Fourteenth Amendment.

Brown v. *Board of Education* put an end to the legal segregation of blacks in American schools. It did not, however, end segregation in fact. Many southerners, and a surprisingly large number of northerners, objected to the removal of racial barriers in the schools. The idea that African-Americans were inferior was something many white Americans could not get rid of quickly. They hated being told they had to associate with people they saw as beneath them. Emotions ran very high. Southern legislatures passed a whole array of laws, many of them unconstitutional, to slow or even halt desegregation in schools. Their tactics were effective, and in 1955 Marshall brought another suit in the Supreme Court asking it to order the states to comply. The Court, in a case often called *Brown II*, issued an order that lower courts were to work out schemes for desegregating southern schools "with all deliberate speed," meaning that southern school districts might be allowed to phase in desegregation over time, but could not stall. Nonetheless, progress was still painfully slow: Ten years after *Brown* v. *Board of Education* only a small percentage of southern students were attending racially mixed schools.

How high emotions could run became clear in Little Rock, Arkansas. The Little Rock Board of Education had worked out in good faith a scheme for the gradual integration of their schools. In the fall of 1957 nine carefully chosen black students—all volunteers—were selected to enter a white high school in Little Rock. These students knew that they would be facing hardships, but were determined to go ahead in order to pave the way for other black students.

Unfortunately, the Arkansas governor, Orval Faubus, who was facing a reelection campaign, decided he could increase his popularity by trying to prevent integration of the high school, which he knew most of his voters opposed. A few days before the opening of the school that fall, Faubus called out the Arkansas National Guard, with the excuse that they were to prevent rioting. In fact, the guardsmen were under orders to turn back the black students.

Eight of the nine students met beforehand and arrived at the school

Governor Orval Faubus of Arkansas opposed the plan to integrate the Little Rock schools in order to increase his popularity with voters, who were mostly against integration. Had Faubus supported integration, it would probably have been done peacefully.

together. They were confronted not only by the guardsmen but by a huge mob of taunting, cursing people. Refused entry to the school, they retreated.

The ninth black student, fifteen-year-old Elizabeth Eckford, had not gotten the message that the students were to travel to the school together. Wearing a brand-new dress she had made for the occasion, she went to school by herself. As she came in sight of the school, the mob gathered there began to shout at her. Seeing the National Guardsmen with their rifles, she felt safe. She walked on, but the guardsmen stopped her. The mob was now cursing at her and about to attack her. She fought her way free of the crowd and got to a bench at a bus stop, where a white newspaper reporter and a white woman helped her get away. The mob scene in front of the Little Rock school was big news. It was carried nightly on television, where Americans watched grown men and women cursing and spitting on teenagers. Many Americans were appalled.

The president at the time was Dwight Eisenhower. He was a decent man, but he had been raised in Kansas, where segregated schools had been the rule, and he had never thought that integration was a good idea. He couldn't decide what to do. However, his advisers told him that he

Elizabeth Eckford, wearing the dress she had made for the occasion walks to school followed by a jeering crowd of whites. Scenes like this, shown on national television, horrified many viewers and increased sympathy for the black cause.

had no choice—the unanimous Supreme Court had said that segregation violated the Constitution, which Eisenhower had sworn to uphold.

Eisenhower met with Governor Faubus. He thought he had Faubus's promise to let integration proceed, but when Faubus went back to Arkansas he continued to keep the black children out of the high school. President Eisenhower felt he had been double-crossed. However, he was still torn. Then Faubus allowed a bunch of thugs to go to the school, where they beat up some black journalists. Soon the mob was out of control. Finally, Eisenhower sent in paratroopers from the 101st Airborne Division, who pushed the mob back at bayonet point. That was not the end of the ordeal for the black students, however. Many white students harassed them, insulted them, tripped them as they went through the halls. But eight of the nine lasted out the year, and in time Little Rock schools were integrated.

Generally, school integration went very slowly through the South. Many school districts continued to resist. Not until the late 1960s, when the civil rights movement rose to a climax, did southern schools really start to integrate.

The situation in the North disclosed some parallels. There segregation was not required by law, but resulted from the fact that blacks mainly lived in their own neighborhoods in big cities and as a matter of course went to their neighborhood schools. Courts ordered some of these

Eventually President Eisenhower sent in troops to protect the black students. Soldiers had to drive away segregationist mobs at bayonet point.

schools to integrate through "busing," that is, a certain number of black students would be taken by bus to white schools, and vice versa. Many whites resisted as they had in the South. In Boston, for example, buses of black students were sometimes stoned by angry whites who did not want to see blacks in schools where their own children went. It would be some time before northern schools were integrated, and as we shall see, by the turn of the century many never were.

CHAPTER III

The Civil Rights Movement Gathers Steam

Schools were not the only area of public life in the South that was segregated: Much else was. Transportation in particular was segregated: African-Americans were required by law to sit in special sections on trains and buses, and to use their own waiting rooms in railroad stations and bus terminals.

In Montgomery, Alabama, the law was somewhat different. Blacks had their own section at the rear of the buses, but if whites filled up the white section, blacks could be asked to give up their seats to allow whites to sit. The bus system was extremely important to blacks in Montgomery, as it was in most southern cities, for it was the only way for many of them to get to work. This was particularly true for black women, most of whom worked in white homes across town as cleaners, laundresses, cooks, child minders. About two-thirds of Montgomery bus riders were black.

On the evening of December 1, 1955, a black woman named Rosa Parks got on a bus to go home from work. She was tired; she worked as a seamstress in a tailor shop, where she also ran a clothes presser. She was not, however, an ordinary woman. She had managed to get more education than most blacks and had even studied in special programs where she had learned about the technique of *passive resistance* used by Mahatma Gandhi in his fight to free India from the British. In this system the protester does not fight, but simply refuses to obey orders.

Rosa Parks had decided that she was going to make a stand the next time she was ordered to give up her seat to a white person. That December evening the bus rapidly filled up. Soon there was no more room in the white section, and Parks was asked to give up her seat. She refused and went on sitting. The bus driver said he would have to have her arrested if she would not give up her seat. Still she refused. The bus driver called the police, who took Rosa Parks to jail.

Very quickly black leaders in Montgomery learned about the incident. Some of them had never been very militant, but others had been waiting for just this chance to make a case. They knew that Parks was a strong, self-reliant woman who could stand up to trouble. She agreed to institute a lawsuit against the bus company. The African-American leaders held some meetings. Soon a young black minister, relatively new to Montgomery, emerged as a natural leader. His name was Martin Luther King Jr. He was no ordinary minister. His parents and some of his grandparents had been fighters for black rights. King had been raised comfortably, had gotten a good education, and had gone into the ministry, a profession that provided much of the black leadership in the South. He, like Parks, was a follower of Gandhi's policy of passive resistance.

King, Parks, and their group decided not only to sue to test the constitutionality of the bus segregation law but to boycott the buses. Without the black riders, the bus system would soon run out of money. Not only did whites also need the buses but white employers needed a way for blacks to get to their jobs. The boycott began. White leaders felt sure that it would not last long. "Comes the first rainy day and the Negroes will be back on the buses," they said. And indeed, in the past blacks had often given in to whites in matters like these.

Rosa Parks sits in a front seat on a bus in Montgomery, Alabama, after the Supreme Court banned segregation in the city's public transit vehicles. A white passenger sits farther back.

But times had changed. World War II was only ten years in the past. Many African-Americans remembered the sacrifices they had made in the war and were determined to win at home. Black leadership was growing bolder. As the bus boycott started, blacks organized carpools to get themselves to work. Black taxi drivers took them in groups, charging low fares. Even white employers, unwilling to do their own cleaning and washing, started driving their cleaning women back and forth to work.

The Montgomery city government struck back. They arrested King, although they soon had to release him. His house was bombed and his mailbox filled with hate mail. By now the bus boycott was getting the attention of the national press. Reporters from northern newspapers, news magazines, and national television came to Montgomery. With so many reporters around, angry whites had to be careful about attacking blacks or trying to intimidate them.

Meanwhile, King and his group had started their lawsuit against the Montgomery bus company. As the bus boycott went on month after month, the case worked its way through the courts. Finally, in November 1956, almost a year after Rosa Parks had refused to give up her seat on the bus, the Supreme Court declared Alabama's bus law unconstitutional. African-Americans could now sit wherever they wanted on Montgomery buses.

The huge press coverage of the Montgomery bus case helped to educate Americans, white and black, about segregation. Many northern whites, only vaguely aware of the inequities of segregation, came to see how unfair it was. Many blacks learned that they could win their fight for civil rights if they were brave and firm.

In 1957 Congress passed a Civil Rights Act aiding blacks in their fight for the vote in the South. In 1960 the act was strengthened by a second Civil Rights Act. With these successes, African-Americans everywhere grew determined to end the inequalities they faced. Early in 1960 some black students at a North Carolina college decided to end segregation in the local lunch counters, using passive resistance. They began "sitting-in" at counters, not causing any trouble, but refusing to leave until they were served. Very quickly the movement spread through the south. The sit-ins badly disrupted business at the lunch counters, and by the end of the year many of them had begun to serve black along with white customers. State laws banning mixed eating places began to fall by the wayside.

Meanwhile, new black organizations, like the Southern Christian Leadership Conference (SCLC), led by Martin Luther King Jr., and the Congress of Racial Equity (CORE) were making themselves felt. In 1961 CORE decided to fight segregation in southern transportation systems. Although the Supreme Court had long since ruled that segregation was illegal in railroad and bus lines that crossed state lines, the ruling had been ignored. James Farmer, head of CORE, organized groups of blacks who traveled from one bus terminal to the next in order to sit-in at waiting rooms. The response from southerners to the "freedom rides" was violent. Buses were met by mobs armed with metal pipes and baseball bats. Many freedom riders (and members of the press) were beaten unconscious. Some were seriously injured; four were murdered. The freedom riders, who included many sympathetic whites, fought on; eventually more than a thousand volunteers were involved. Within a few years the battle had been won. Trains, buses, waiting rooms, hotels and motels—all must be open to everyone on an equal basis.

Black students sit in at a counter in a drug store in Helena, Arkansas. Although they would not be served, they occupied seats that otherwise might have been taken by white customers, thus hurting business. Store owners soon began to give way.

Legally, African-Americans could vote. The Fifteenth Amendment to the U.S. Constitution was passed in 1875 specifically to ensure that right. Blacks were the majority in some southern counties, a large minority in others, and if they voted they could change things. However, as we have seen, for generations whites had kept them from registering to vote through trickery and intimidation. For example, in some places literacy tests were given to people who wanted to register. A white person might be asked to read a simple newspaper article, while a black one might be given a complicated legal document. If all else failed, blacks trying to vote would be threatened with a beating, and sometimes got one—or worse.

The voter registration movement of the 1960s ran into the same resistance the freedom riders had faced. There was violence, more beatings, and even deaths. Unfortunately, the FBI was then headed by the legendary J. Edgar Hoover, highly popular with the public, who often ran the FBI as if it were his private police force. Hoover was very much against the black activists. Moreover, many of his agents in the South were themselves southerners. As a result, FBI agents frequently stood around taking notes while mobs beat freedom riders and interfered with blacks trying to register.

Without protection from the federal government the violence could not be stopped. In September 1962 a federal court ordered the University of Mississippi to admit an African-American applicant, James Meredith. There was a riot in which two people were killed. The next year segregationists blew up a black church, killing four little girls. But perhaps the worst violence came in 1963 in Birmingham, Alabama. That city was considered by blacks to be the most determined to maintain segregation. A group of black leaders, including Martin Luther King Jr., led African-Americans in demonstrations against segregation there. City authorities fought back, slamming the demonstrators with water from high-pressure hoses and threatening them with clubs and vicious dogs.

These events all got widespread coverage on television, in magazines,

Right: Southern police and sheriffs attacked demonstrators and freedom marchers with dogs, clubs, and high-pressure hoses. Here two demonstrators leap to escape the force of high-pressure fire hoses.

Below: Demonstrators and marchers were frequently beaten by segregationist mobs; sometimes they were murdered. Martin Luther King Jr. holds up photographs of three young Civil Rights workers, two of them white volunteers from the North, who had been murdered and their bodies buried by bulldozers.

One important event in the Civil Rights movement was a march, led by King, from Selma to Montgomery, Alabama, the state capital. Marchers arrived at Montgomery on March 25, 1965.

and newspapers. Americans, watching blacks being attacked by club-wielding southern sheriffs nightly on their television screens were appalled. African-American leaders and increasing numbers of whites pressed President John F. Kennedy to do something. A mass march on Washington was called, and on August 28, 1963, 250,000 people gathered at the Lincoln Memorial. They heard King give one of the most memorable speeches of twentieth-century America. He closed by saying, "I have a dream," that one day, "all of God's children . . . will be able to join hands and sing . . . . Free at last! Free at last! Thank God Almighty, we are free at last!"

Kennedy now put his weight behind a strong civil rights bill that prohibited segregation in public places, forbade racial discrimination in employment, and established machinery to ensure that African-Americans could actually vote. On November 22, 1963, while the civil rights bill was still being considered by Congress, President Kennedy was assassinated by an emotionally disturbed man named Lee Harvey Oswald. Kennedy's vice president, Lyndon B. Johnson, announced immediately that he would continue the fight for the civil rights bill. On the strength of the national emotion over Kennedy's death, Johnson in 1964 was able to get the bill passed. In 1965 a second bill strengthened black voting rights. The battle was far from over, but the southern states now understood that they had the federal government against them, and things slowly improved for blacks.

However, white sympathy for American blacks may have been set back by the activities of some very militant—even violent—black organi-

A key moment in American history came with the 1963 March on Washington, where King made his historic "I Had a Dream" speech. King is shown waving to the crowd as he delivers the speech.

zations. One of these was called the Black Panthers. They were responsible for a number of deaths, not only among their adversaries but also of some of their own members thought to be disloyal.

The most influential of the black militants was the leader of a minority faction of a religious sect called the Nation of Islam, usually referred to as the Black Muslims. This was Malcolm Little, who referred to himself as Malcolm X in order to avoid a name given his family by whites in the days of slavery. Malcolm X developed a large following of militant African-Americans who proclaimed they would use any means necessary to bring about fair and equal conditions in America. Malcolm X was seen by white Americans as a real threat and more or less demonized. In 1965 he was assassinated by members of the majority faction of the Muslims. By that time, however, Malcolm X had softened his views about whites and was calling for improved race relations. In the late 1990s this one-time "black terror" was honored with his portrait on a U.S. postage stamp.

Although the activities of the most militant African-Americans may have antagonized many whites, the work of nonviolent groups like the NAACP, the SCLC, and SNCC (student nonviolent coordinating committee) was very effective. They had brought about the improvement of the quality of life for black Americans in many ways, often dramatically so. For instance, in 1968 there were five blacks in Congress; in 2001 there were thirty-six. In 1967 Thurgood Marshall was appointed the first black person on the Supreme Court. African-Americans became mayors, senators, and members of the president's cabinet. By the turn of the century blacks were earning huge sums of money as athletes and entertainers; and in many cases climbing to the top in business and the professions.

In 1960, 42 percent of blacks were below the poverty line; by 2000, 24 percent were. In 1966, 4 percent of blacks were college graduates; in 2000, it was 17 percent (29 percent of whites were college graduates). Between 1972 and 1992 the number of black-owned businesses tripled.

Overall, about a third of African-American families had moved into the middle class by the year 2000.

The change for blacks in the second half of the twentieth century was dramatic. Nonetheless, they lagged behind in some areas. For example, in 1997 median income for a family of four was $34,800 for blacks, $56,000 for whites. Blacks did not live as long and generally had poorer health.

Part of the problem was that large numbers of blacks were trapped in *cycles of poverty* in inner cities. That is, young black males raised in poverty, often without fathers, tended to drop out of school or use drugs, and then burden some teenage girl with his children; the teenage mothers, of course, had to care for the children without any financial or emotional support from the fathers. Poorly educated, with life complicated by children, these young people found it difficult to get any but the lowest-paying jobs. Many teenage girls went on to raise children as single parents on welfare checks, children who would repeat the pattern. The nation's city schools became increasingly segregated as suburban towns made it difficult for any but the affluent to buy houses, and middle-class whites left the cities. Thus, by the turn of the century many American children went to schools in which they rarely—in some places never—had a classmate of a different race.

Thus, while it is true that blacks have made great progress in American society and enjoy the same freedom as whites, it is also true that they lag behind economically. The gap is being closed, but only slowly.

CHAPTER IV

The Upheavals of the 1960s

The "1960s" is a term commonly used for the massive changes in attitudes that came over the American people in the years from, roughly, 1965 to 1973. Some of these changes in ways of thinking and doing quickly disappeared, but others of them have helped to shape the United States that exists today.

Four movements stand out: the counterculture movement of the so-called hippies, which brought new attitudes toward sex, drugs, and how life should be lived; the peace movement, which helped to end the Vietnam War; the environmental protection movement, which fought to stop pollution and save the wilderness; and the women's movement, which tried to increase the presence of women in business, the professions, and government.

These movements were all related. Many of the people who favored—or opposed—one of these causes, also supported, or opposed, others. Clearly, people who wish to spare lives lost in war are likely to feel strongly about protecting other kinds of life on earth.

It is sometimes believed that the members of the counterculture were at the heart of all of these movements. That is not entirely correct; much

The counterculture believed in love, the free expression of emotion, and unconventional clothes and hairstyles. However, their ideals often proved unrealistic: this 1968 love-in held in Los Angeles ended with fighting between celebrants and police.

of the leadership and effort in these movements came from mainstream Americans, many of whom did not approve of counterculture ideas or lifestyle. Nonetheless, the counterculture hippies usually strongly favored the antiwar effort and the environmental cause, if not always the women's movement.

The term *counter* means against; *culture* is the whole set of beliefs, folkways, customs, ways of thinking and doing things that a nation follows. The counterculture of the 1960s, which actually had its greatest effects later, was a movement determined to replace the American culture of the postwar era with a new—and its promoters thought—better one.

America had been visited by earlier counterculture movements. In particular, in the early decades of the twentieth century, a movement had arisen to throw off the strident morality of the Victorian nineteenth century which had started out as a call for order and decency, but had become overly repressive, inhibiting spontaneity and creating straitjackets of middle-class manners. This earlier counterculture had wanted people to live freer, more expressive lives. The effect was to establish an ethic that put the *individual* first, instead of the needs of the community.

The counterculture of the 1960s did not grow directly out of this earlier movement, but it was similar in that it pushed the idea of the freedom of the individual to an extreme. It began during World War II, when a tiny handful of rebels at Columbia University in New York City developed a philosophy that held that there was no such thing as right or wrong, good or bad: People ought to be free to try out any kind of experience they felt like.

This tiny group was led by the novelist Jack Kerouac and the poet Allen Ginsberg. They began to experiment with sex, drugs, even crime. They were at first too tiny a group to have any impact, but in 1957 Kerouac's novel *On the Road* was published to much publicity, and Ginsberg's poem "Howl" was banned in some places, generating more publicity. Kerouac had named the group the Beat Generation, and its fol-

Beat poet Allen Ginsberg (left) with Timothy Leary, who advocated the use of LSD as a way to reach a "higher consciousness." Ginsberg, too, favored the use of drugs, no limitations on sex, or indeed on any other kind of behavior as long as it was peaceful. Both of these men were important in setting the hippy philosophy.

lowers were dubbed *beatniks*, or the *Beats*. Press interest was high, and many young people read "Howl" and *On the Road*, which expressed the Beat philosophy of living without rules. Many of the basic ideas of the counterculture of the 1960s grew out of the Beat movement.

Historians usually date the beginning of the counterculture wave to the "free speech" movement at the University of California in Berkeley, outside San Francisco. In 1964 some students at Berkeley demonstrated against new restrictions on distributing political pamphlets from tables just outside the campus. The university tried to prevent these demonstrations. The protest movement grew. The university called in police and soon the campus was in turmoil. Many professors supported the students'

Mario Savio emerged as the leader of the so-called free speech movement at the University of California's Berkeley campus. He speaks in this picture to a rally of more than 3,500 people, mostly students.

ideas, in particular their demand for free speech, by which they meant the right to demonstrate, put up signs, publish pamphlets and newsletters.

The movement was contagious. Students on other campuses started their own protests on various issues, and soon a number of ideas began to coalesce. These ideas were quite varied and sometimes contradictory. The people in the movement, sometimes called *hippies*, said that was all right: people should follow their feelings, and if their feelings were sometimes contradictory, so be it. As the saying went, people should "do their own thing." (*Hip* was an old jazz musicians' term for "knowing" or "aware." A hippie was thus an underground insider.)

But this was a counterculture. The hippies were, by philosophy, opposed to anything and everything the mainstream culture stood for. If Americans believed in being neat and tidy, the hippies would dress in frayed and dirty clothes. If the main culture said that sex should be confined to marriage, the hippies would insist on complete sexual freedom. If most Americans shuddered at the idea of drugs, the hippies would build a lifestyle around them. If the mainstream admired hard work and getting ahead, the hippies would work only as much as they had to and spend the rest of the time having fun. These two ideas—a belief in feelings rather than thought as a guide to behavior and a rejection of the mainstream culture—were central to the counterculture movement of the 1960s.

The counterculture was made up of often unrelated strands, often with opposing goals. In many cases, the ideals and projects taken up by the young people of the counterculture were unrealistic and doomed to failure. Among these were the communes. As had happened in the United States before, some of the hippies wanted to create their own self-sufficient communities where they could shut themselves off from the mainstream culture and develop their own alternative lifestyle. Communes sprang up mainly in areas where cheap land was available, or, in a few cases, in low-rent districts in big cities. These communes had differing plans and philosophies but in general they wanted their members to be

A typical commune scene. The hippies on most communes believed they should work only as much as absolutely necessary. They also felt that their way of life was a statement against what they saw as the conformity and rigidity of mainstream life. There were, however, negatives: this commune suffered an outbreak of hepatitis because of poor sanitary conditions.

free to think, act, dress as they wished. There would be only the barest minimum of rules, none if possible. It was hoped that members would see what needed to be done and would chop wood, plant gardens, tend children, and wash dishes of their own accord, without being told. They also believed that they were setting an example of how to live for the rest of the world.

There was, however, a basic contradiction built into the commune idea—individualism as opposed to community responsibility. On one hand, the members were only supposed to do what they felt like doing; on the other hand, wood had to be cut, corn planted, children bathed. Suppose nobody felt like doing such things?

That, very frequently, was what happened. Many communes suddenly found themselves running short of food or out of wood in the middle of winter. They quickly disintegrated. Others, feeling that they ought to welcome all comers, took in a lot of people who were merely looking for free food and shelter and contributed nothing to the community. In still others, members, believing that they were free to do as they liked, used a lot of drugs and nothing ever got done. A few of these communes continue to exist into the twenty-first century, but they have carried on only because, like the rest of the world, they decided they had to be properly organized, with rules to be followed.

We should bear in mind that the counterculture hippies, particularly the more extreme of them, were a small minority of Americans. Probably not more than ten thousand people ever committed themselves to commune life for as long as a year. The hard core of hippies probably constituted fewer than a half million people, only a small percentage of even college-age people. A considerably larger number of people, however, agreed with this or that aspect of the counterculture philosophy. Probably the majority supported greater sexual freedoms than the laws, generally ignored anyway, allowed. Others believed that marijuana ought to be legalized; still others though there might be something to the commune idea.

But, taken as a whole, the counterculture was disliked by the majority of Americans and hated by a good many others. It seemed to them that the hippies were often hypocritical and self-indulgent: Under the guise of saving the world, many hippies seemed to be trying to have fun without working very hard. There was, further, a dark side to the counterculture: Too many people were damaged, or even died, from drugs; too many children were born to young parents not much interested in raising them; and in some cases, as among the so-called "flower children" of San Francisco's Haight-Ashbury hippie district, there were drug-related murders.

Nonetheless, by the late 1960s there was widespread interest in the counterculture ideas among the young, not merely college students, but down into the high schools and even junior high schools. A critically important factor in raising this interest was a new form of popular music, at first called *rock and roll*, and then shortened to *rock*. This music had grown out of a combination of jazz, 1940s swing, the so-called Chicago blues of African-Americans and, most immediately, the black rhythm-and-blues of the 1940s and early 1950s. Soon a version of rhythm-and-blues gained young white audiences, and performers like Elvis Presley became immensely popular. In 1964 the Beatles, a British group, made an American

Rock and roll became the theme music for the youth culture, and in time the main popular music for America. Elvis Presley, shown here in 1970 in his famous white suit, was one of the earliest rock stars.

tour, drawing an enormous following with their own less intense version of rock. With a strong beat and simple melodies, the lyrics of many of these rock tunes promoted counterculture ideas in favor of drugs and teenage sex, and against the mainstream culture. There was also a growing interest in folk music, which took as subjects the plight of blacks, workers, and other social causes. But folk music never had the popularity of rock, which very soon became the basic popular music for the young. Fifty years after the birth of rock, it was still firmly on the side of the counterculture.

The members of the counterculture were among the first to oppose the Vietnam War—the men among them, after all, were the ones who would have to kill or be killed in it. But many mainstream Americans had begun to oppose the Vietnam War quite early, too, and in the end it was the opposition of ordinary Americans that forced the government to find a solution.

The country of Vietnam had been divided into a Communist north and a capitalist south as a consequence of events during and after World War II. Neither government was democratic, but the government of South Vietnam was particularly corrupt. A Communist-led rebellion broke out against it. The rebels in South Vietnam were soon joined by troops from North Vietnam. The United States government was committed to a policy of containing communism, and decided to aid South Vietnam. At first, the aid consisted only of arms, but in 1961 President Kennedy began to send in troops, and his successor, Lyndon Johnson, increased them until there were 500,000 servicemen there, most of them draftees. The fighting was inconclusive, and by the mid-1960s millions of Americans were deciding that a great deal of blood was being shed for no good reason: Americans ought to get out of Vietnam. (The Vietnam War is discussed in the volume in this series called *The United States in the Cold War, 1945–1991*.) Young people, not all of them members of the counterculture, protested on campuses, picketed military installa-

An exhausted marine in camouflage paint expresses the distaste both the fighting men and the people back home came to have for the Vietnam War. By 1968 the majority of Americans were opposed to the war, and morale among the soldiers was low.

Students on many campuses demonstrated against the war. At Kent State University in Ohio in 1970 National Guardsmen were brought in to control the demonstrations. Some guardsmen opened fire and four students were killed. Events like these did much to discredit the war.

tions, burned their draft cards, and in some instances fled to Canada or elsewhere to escape a draft that would force them to risk death or to kill others in a cause they believed to be wrong.

But it was hardly just the young: prominent figures like Martin Luther King Jr., and the famous baby doctor Benjamin Spock, spoke out against the war. In the end, it was television, not the counterculture, that turned public opinion. As the debate grew, news shows increased their coverage of the war, and Americans began to see on their screens each night the brutalized bodies of soldiers and sometimes of children. By 1968, when President Johnson was facing reelection, the war had become so unpopular that Johnson knew he could not win another term and decided against running. His vice president, Hubert Humphrey got the Democratic nomination but lost to Richard Nixon who became president on a promise to find "peace with honor."

One result of the antiwar movement was the introduction of an amendment to the Constitution that would lower the voting age from twenty-one to eighteen. The idea was that if young men were required to risk their lives in Vietnam, they ought to have the right to vote. The twenty-sixth Amendment easily passed Congress and was ratified by the states in 1971. While the law seemed just, it had little practical effect; youthful citizens were less likely to vote than older ones and usually voted much as the older ones around them did.

Environmentalism, although it was generally supported by the counterculture, was also a mainstream movement. Concern for the environment was hardly new. Several presidents, especially Theodore Roosevelt in the first decade of the twentieth century, had pushed hard for the creation of national parks and forest preserves. Millions of Americans had always been concerned about the extermination of the buffalo, the cutting down of forests, and other violations of the environment.

Perhaps the most important factor in reawakening the environmental movement was the publication in 1962 of Rachel Carson's book

Silent Spring, which explained the dangers of pesticides to wildlife. As a result, forty states and the federal government outlawed the use of the chemical DDT. Other environmentalists tried to prevent the construction of an eight-hundred-mile pipeline across Alaska, lobbied against commercial uses of wildlife sanctuaries, and stopped the development of the SST, a supersonic airplane whose flights would damage the earth's ozone layer. President Nixon authorized the Alaska pipeline; but on the other hand, he supported the creation of a federal Environmental Protection Agency. Later presidents used the National Environmental Policy Act of 1969 and other legislation to extend protections to mil-

Recycling began to be widely adopted in the 1970s, and by the year 2000 was required by many cities and towns. A woman bundles newspapers to go to the recycling center.

lions of acres of national parks, coastal zones, wildlife refuges, and endangered species of animals.

Since the 1960s some presidents have been supporters of environmental protection, others have been opposed. The government of Ronald Reagan, for example, preferred to see national parks and natural lands generally exploited for commercial purposes—the trees cut to supply lumber, the ground drilled for oil. This also, generally speaking, was the position of the two Presidents Bush. President Bill Clinton, on the other hand, added millions of acres of natural lands to the protected lists. Broadly speaking, the majority of Americans came to favor protecting the environment, although they might disagree about what should be protected, and how.

Of all the movements that blossomed in the 1960s, the one that may have had the most profound effect on American life was the women's movement. Before the twentieth century women could not vote in most states, and were barred by law, tradition, or both, from practicing the professions or rising in the ranks of business. In some states they could not serve on juries, and until World War II, they were barred from the armed forces. Most jobs open to women were menial ones such as domestic servants, laundresses, or on assembly lines. Women were generally paid less than men for the same job. The only white-collar jobs completely open to women were as librarians, teachers, nurses, and secretaries, although some did manage to get into the professions as doctors and lawyers. It was rare for women to be school superintendents, despite the fact that most teachers were women.

There had been earlier women's movements, especially in the nineteenth century. By 1919 women had gained the vote, and large numbers were going to college and entering the professions. By the 1940s a significant number of American women were college educated. They were restless and frustrated at not being able to use their educations for anything but taking care of their homes and children. In 1963 one of these

The feminist movement was not an invention of the 1960s but had roots deep in the past. In 1923 feminists such as the famous poet Edna St. Vincent Millay (left) appeared in Washington to state the women's case. By 1971 women's clothing had changed considerably, but the message was the same: equality with men now.

unhappy housewives, Betty Friedan, published *The Feminine Mystique*, which expressed these frustrations. The book revived the feminist movement. New feminist organizations like the National Organization for Women (NOW) were formed.

Congress, recognizing that women were the majority of voters, quickly passed the Equal Pay Act in 1963 and the next year extended to women the protections against discrimination that had been granted to African-Americans. However, an effort to pass an Equal Rights Amendment to the Constitution failed, for a variety of reasons.

Nevertheless, women made great strides. In 1973 there were only fifteen women in the House of Representatives and none in the Senate; by 2000 there were fifty-seven female representatives and nine female senators. In 1900 only 1 percent of lawyers were women; a century later it was 29 percent

However, the women's movement was not alone in moving women into the workplace. For one thing, many Americans wanted the things that the industrial machine was able to turn out; women with children went to work to bring in extras their families could not otherwise have. Increasing numbers of single mothers found that they had to work whether they wanted to or not. Finally, jobs opened up to women that had been closed before simply because in these years of a strong economy there were not enough men to fill them. Should large numbers of women decide to leave the workforce, the gross national product would drop sharply, with fewer consumer goods for all. As a consequence of all this, the percentage of married women working outside the home jumped from 6 percent in 1900 to nearly half by 2000.

Women have made particularly great progress in sports. Before the 1960s, aside from a few then secondary sports like figure skating, sports was dominated by men. Except in golf, tennis, field hockey, and softball girls were expected to stay on the sidelines as cheerleaders. In 1972 Congress passed laws requiring schools and colleges to give women better sports programs. By 2000 women's professional basketball leagues were flourishing, and tennis stars like Martina Hingis and Serena Williams were shining brightly and earning fortunes. There were amateur leagues for ice-hockey, soccer, and lacrosse; and women were competing as NASCAR drivers.

Nonetheless, males continued to dominate in sports, government, industry. In part this was because millions of Americans continued to stick to traditional values, which require that women be, first and foremost, good wives and mothers. In part this was due to the simple fact that women, not men, give birth to children, nurse them, and tend to feel more comfortable caring for babies than men do and thus interrupt their careers in ways men do not. And no doubt there remained many men who continued to feel uncomfortable working alongside women, or having them as their superiors on the job. Certainly, few of them wanted to stay home to clean and cook and care for small children.

The ideas that came boiling up in the 1960s, spurring on these movements, amounted to a rebellion in attitude. Some of the strands in these movements had little long-term effects. The commune movement died out almost entirely. The antiwar movement ended with the close of the Vietnam War.

But other ideas that surfaced in the 1960s have had tremendous effects on America. For one, before the 1960s only a tiny minority of Americans had ever used drugs; today drug use is commonplace. Arguments continue over what place drugs ought to have in American society, but there is no doubt that they have damaged, and in some cases destroyed, millions of American lives, as the cases of athletes like the baseball stars Doc Gooden and Darryl Strawberry have shown.

For another, although there was always some debate, the idea that the environment ought to be protected became widely accepted. Recycling, lead-free gasoline, lead-free paint, and much else became part of everyday life in America.

Perhaps most significant are changing attitudes toward sex and the family. As we have seen, before the 1960s a woman who gave birth before she was married was often disgraced; and while it is certainly true that many women had sex before marriage by about 1950, perhaps as many as half still did not. (It was accepted that most men would have sex before marriage.) By the year 2000 the single mother was commonplace. In part this had to do with the sexual freedoms promoted by the counterculture, which resulted in many women having unplanned children whose fathers were not interested in caring for them. In part it was a consequence of the idea that women should be able to get along happily without men, which many feminists, although by no means all, believed.

The acceptance of the single-parent family, in most instances a fatherless one, is a change of great magnitude. Throughout history the nuclear family of father, mother, and children has been a central—many think, *the* central—institution in human society. Nobody is quite sure what the long-term consequences of the fatherless family will be. However, a substantial number of studies have shown that while many single mothers raise successful children, on average, children without fathers at home do less well in school, in their jobs, and in their marriages. But time alone will tell.

CHAPTER V

The March of Science

Many young people, seeing the late-twentieth-century advances in technology, particularly in electronic communication, believed that they were living through the great age of scientific invention. In truth, historians believe that the second half of the 1800s, when the telephone, wireless communication, recorded sound, the movies, the automobile, the airplane, the electric motor, and much else were developed, deserves that title. Nonetheless, there is no denying that huge strides in technology were made during the second half of the twentieth century. (The study of nineteenth-century technology is told in the volume in this series called *The Rise of Industry*.)

Many of the technological improvements were driven by World War II of 1939 to 1945, during which both sides pushed their scientists to produce better weapons systems, better airplanes, better medical treatment for the wounded, and more. The most famous of these developments was atomic power. Things in the world around us are made up of atoms—hydrogen atoms, copper atoms, and so forth. It had long been known that the elements in atoms were held together by a terrific force. If the atom could be broken apart, or "split," a great deal of energy would be released. If the release of energy was uncontrolled, a huge explosion would result.

In 1939 some American scientists, aware that the Germans—soon to be an enemy in World War II—were searching for a way to split the atom, asked Albert Einstein, a German refugee and the most famous mathematician in the world, to write president Franklin Roosevelt about the possibility of an atomic bomb. Roosevelt soon established a secret task force, known as the Manhattan Project, to build the bomb. In the summer of 1945 such a bomb was successfully tested, and soon two bombs were dropped on the Japanese cities of Hiroshima and Nagasaki. Scientists also knew that if this atomic reaction was allowed to proceed in a controlled way, the energy produced would come in the form of heat, which could be used to run huge steam generators for making electricity. By the 1950s atomic energy plants were being built in most industrial nations. Today such plants exist everywhere—in 1998, 19 percent of American electricity was produced by atomic power.

However, there are drawbacks to atomic power. For one thing, atomic power plants produce very dangerous radioactive material that can last for hundreds or even thousands of years. This radioactive waste is hard to dispose of. For another, an accident at an atomic energy plant, releasing radioactive materials into the air, can endanger life even at a great distance. An accident at a Russian plant at the city of Chernobyl in 1986 not only killed many people near the plant but sent radioactive material around the world.

Yet those favoring atomic energy say that such plants do not create the kind of pollution produced by coal- and oil-burning plants and have the potential to supply an almost unlimited amount of cheap energy, which would be of great help to humanity, especially in the poorer areas of the world.

A second area in which wartime pressures pushed technology forward was in space exploration. Through most of the war, airplanes had

Atomic energy may yet prove to be the answer to the use of coal and oil to create power, which pollute the atmosphere. However, it is too risky. These children are suffering from radiation poisoning caused by the accident at the Chernobyl atomic energy plant in Ukraine, even though they lived 350 miles away.

been powered by propellers, using the ancient principle of the screw. However, it had long been known that in theory planes could be powered by jet propulsion, the force that pushes Fourth of July rockets into the air. During World War II scientists on both sides worked feverishly to develop effective jet planes and rockets. The Germans got there first, and as the war was winding down, began firing the infamous V-2 rockets into London. The development of jet power proceeded rapidly; by the 1960s jet planes were pushing propeller-driven planes aside, although propellers continued to be used on smaller aircraft.

It was jet flight, however, that made it possible to send vehicles into space. In 1957 the Soviet Union sent the first of its *Sputnik* satellites into space, and followed with an announcement that it had produced a jet-propelled missile powerful enough to reach the United States. In a near panic, the United States redoubled its efforts to produce its own space satellites and missiles, and in 1958 it sent *Explorer* and *Vanguard* into orbit around the world. Soon it caught up to the Soviets in missile production.

President Eisenhower and Congress had established the National Aeronautical and Space Agency (NASA) in 1958 to oversee American space programs. Then, five days after his inauguration on January 20, 1961, John F. Kennedy challenged Congress to provide the funds—eventually over $24 billion—that the American scientific community needed to develop the technology to send a man to the moon and return him

The principle of the jet engine had been known for a long time, but not until World War II did scientists figure out how to make it practical. This V-2 bomb, being tested in New Mexico, was one of the earliest devices to use jet power. Today most large airplanes, space vehicles, and missiles are jet-driven.

safely. To most Americans, this was a project out of science fiction. But Kennedy's challenge was inspirational. The space program was already under way, and four months after Kennedy's challenge, Alan Shepard was launched into space. John Glenn orbited the globe in 1962. Then Neil Armstrong and Edwin Aldrin walked on the moon in July 1969, an event that tied together two great technological developments of the postwar era—space exploration and television. Tens of millions of Americans sat glued to their TVs watching live as Armstrong stepped onto the moon and said, "That's one small step for a man, one giant leap for mankind."

This photograph of astronaut Buzz Aldrin climbing down to the surface of the moon was taken by his partner, Neil Armstrong, who had already descended. Without jet power space explorations such as this one would not have been possible.

These space ventures, however, are extraordinarily expensive. In the 1960s NASA was spending as much as $5 billion a year, as much as the federal government was contributing to schools at the time. Many felt that the money could be better spent on earth rather than in space. Others answered that the space program produced side benefits in new technologies valuable for both military and peaceful purposes.

The technological development that may have had more impact on American society than any other was the invention of television. TV had been technically possible since the 1920s, but not until about 1950 did significant numbers of American homes have television—5 million that year, with the numbers rapidly growing. At first, television was black and white, but color technology improved and by the 1960s most Americans were switching over. Cable was available in the 1950s, but it only became widely used in the 1970s. The VCR was introduced in about 1980 and by 1992, 77 percent of television owners also had a VCR. By the turn of the century, 99 percent of American homes had color television sets, many of them had two or three. Despite the advent of cable and the VCR, regular television programming remained dominant into 2000. The big network sit-coms still got the heaviest regular audiences, although major sports events like the Superbowl, and big news stories like the Gulf War, often drew huge numbers of people.

Television has had a tremendous effect on American culture, to the point that it now dominates the free time of Americans. It is difficult for young people today to realize that before, say, 1920, most people enjoyed professional entertainment only occasionally, in the form of a theatrical show, a concert, or a sporting event. Most entertainment was home-made—a card game, a sing around the parlor piano, a horseshoe-throwing match. With the coming of radio and the movies in the first half of the twentieth century, the time spent with the media increased: A young person might see a movie once or twice a week, listen to an hour of radio shows in the afternoon or evening. But those hours spent in passive enter-

Early television sets were big and cumbersome. In most homes there was one set in the living room, shared by all. In this scene from the 1950s, a housewife watches television while tending her baby and ironing clothes. Television helped women to get through the routine tasks of housekeeping.

tainment were nothing to what came with TV. Television simply soaked up Americans' spare time. By 1960 Americans were watching 28 hours of television a week, and the figure continued to rise; in 2000 families had their TVs on forty-four hours a week and individuals spent more time looking at them than they spent at work or at school.

Another major effect of television has been to take over delivery of the news. In 1967 almost three-quarters of Americans read a newspaper everyday; by 1993 it was down to half, and for younger readers it was less than a third. Television is particularly important to politicians. In 1960, during the first presidential debate, John F. Kennedy, who had recently had the benefit of the California sun, appeared fresh and youthful; his opponent, Richard M. Nixon, had been ill with a virus and appeared haggard. Those who heard the debate on radio believed Nixon had done well; those who saw it on television thought that Kennedy was an easy victor. Kennedy won the election by a slim margin. Similarly, President Reagan, a trained actor, impressed people with his television appearances, even though his facts were sometimes wrong; television made this former actor one of the most popular American presidents of the twentieth century. Indeed, television advertising has become essential to electioneering. It is so expensive that candidates must spend as much or even more time raising money as they do actually giving speeches and meeting people. Inevitably, they owe favors to the institutions and individuals who have given them large sums of money.

That television has much of value to offer is unquestioned; but that it often fails to live up to its potential is widely agreed by those who have studied it carefully. One complaint concerns the presentation of news. Television is a visual medium, and producers of news shows usually give more space to news events for which they have good pictures than to more important stories. Thus, a story about a fire with shots of flames crackling from windows will get more space than a terrible drought involving millions of people for which there are only pictures of parched fields.

For another, in order to attract large audiences, television news plays up scandals involving celebrities or macabre murders, once again at the expense of important decisions of the Supreme Court or new laws passed by Congress. Finally, a television news show only skims over the top of a story, frequently failing to give viewers an idea of its true significance. Av Weston, who worked for television news shows for years, says, "You can't substitute a headline for a full account. We always leave things out."

If television has had dramatic effects on American life, to young people a more recent change has been the new "information technology"—

that is, computers. The first electronic computers were developed in the late 1930s and 1940s, but only in the late 1970s and early 1980s did practical personal computers become available. Their reduction in size and increase in efficiency has been astonishing. Millions of ordinary Americans routinely use computers far more powerful than what was available to the most advanced scientists only a few decades earlier. It has been said that if the automobile industry had developed as quickly, by 2000 cars would have had engines a tenth of an inch long and would have cost $4.00. In 1992 only a quarter of American homes had computers; by the turn of the century it was over half. Teenagers today average about two hours a day at their computers, playing games, doing homework, and sending and receiving e-mail. (The boom in cell phones came even quicker, from 5 million in use in 1990 to over 70 million in 2000.)

This Eniac, the first true computer, was less powerful than many laptops owned by students today but took up a whole room.

While the computer has proven critically important to many new developments in science, medicine, and elsewhere, and is certainly widely used by students to collect information, its main use has been for entertainment, not merely in the form of video games but for Internet browsing, visiting chat rooms, and the like.

Taken together, the new technological devices in American homes, like television, the computer, and more, have changed American life. Principally, people tend to interact less with each other and more with machines. Instead of playing cards, Ping-Pong, gossiping over coffee in the kitchen, arguing about politics, or reading stories to children, they are browsing the Net, sending e-mail, and, most particularly, watching television. These are different kinds of experiences from interacting with people. Obviously, what a person says or does has no effect on the television characters as it has with real people. Even exchanging e-mail is quite different from talking to somebody, where you see their expressions, hear their feelings in their voices. At the beginning of the twenty-first century, personal physical contact among Americans of all ages was markedly reduced because of the new technologies.

CHAPTER VI

The Changing Character of America

The United States that existed in the millennium year of 2000 was different from the one that existed at the end of World War II in 1945. For one thing, despite moments of recession, like that in the 1970s, American prosperity continued to grow at an astonishing rate. The 1990s in particular saw year after year of growth without a halt. The wealth of ordinary families was amazing. In the 1950s there were 3.75 people for each car in the United States—just about one car for each family, which means that many families didn't have a car while others had two. It was rare for teenagers to own cars. In 1977 the figure was one car for each two people, which meant that the two-car family was a norm; many families had three cars or more.

In the 1950s Americans were acquiring still-novel, and quite expensive, black-and-white television sets; by the 1900s, as we have seen, most homes had more than one color set, along with the VCRs and cable systems. In the 1950s most families had a single radio and phonograph in the living room, which the family shared. By the year 2000 even quite young children had their own personal CD and tape players, and in many cases their own television sets in their own rooms.

In the 1950s travel by airplane was too expensive for ordinary people; even Hollywood film stars often traveled from New York to California by train. Trips to Europe or Asia were almost always made by ship. By the end of the century even young children routinely flew, sometimes by themselves, between cities to visit relatives. And, as we have said earlier, between 1950 and 2000 the per capita gross national product tripled, meaning that every young person could have three times as many "things" as his or her grandparents had had when they were growing up.

Nonetheless, along with prosperity, inequities of wealth were also growing. Generally, everybody had grown more prosperous, but some had gained more than others. The gap between the rich, the middle class, and the poor had widened. In 1949 the bottom 20 percent of families received 4.5 percent of the nation's income, while the top 5 percent received 16.9 percent. In 1997

American prosperity is symbolized by the huge array of choices available to ordinary American people in shops and stores.

the bottom group had 4.2 percent, while the top had 20.3 percent. Thus, the poorest fifth of Americans were now earning a slightly smaller share of the national wealth than they had fifty years earlier, while the top fifth was taking in a 2 percent larger share. Those in the middle were receiving about the same slice of the pie as they had before.

One reason for this growing disparity in wealth was a rising tide of immigration because immigrants usually start out poor. The United States had seen a massive inflow of immigrants from about 1830 to 1920. Most of these earlier immigrants were German, Irish, Italian, Polish, and Jews from Eastern Europe, although almost every nation in the world was represented. After unusually high rates at the turn of the century,

The immigrants of the 1800s and early 1900s came mostly from Europe, although there were a few from Asia as well. Many of the European immigrants came through Ellis Island, where they were given physical examinations.

immigration was drastically slowed in the 1920s and 1930s due to restrictive laws and other causes, such as war and depression.

During the years from 1920 to 1970 most of the children and grandchildren of this vast wave of immigrants were *assimilated* into American society. That is, although they might keep to old religious practices and maintain some folkways, such as the polkas danced at Polish weddings, or the blintzes and lox eaten by Jews on festive occasions, by the 1960s the descendants of the older immigrants had mainly forgotten the languages of their grandparents and had begun to act and think like all other Americans. Increasingly, they married outside their own group, which by itself made it harder for them to hang on to old ways: In 1910 only 1 percent of Jews married non-Jews; by 2000 it was 50 percent.

This assimilation occurred in part because there were no longer such large numbers of new immigrants arriving to draw earlier ones back into their ethnic groups. That is, new immigrants tended to settle in ethnic neighborhoods where they continued to speak their old languages, followed their old customs in dress and behavior. So long as their ethnic neighborhoods existed, the children of older immigrants were inclined to remain in them. But when the influx of German, Jewish, Italian, and other immigrants slowed, these ethnic neighborhoods began to disappear as younger generations moved away, especially to the ethnically mixed suburbs where everybody spoke English, went to the same schools, belonged to the same bowling leagues and businessmen's clubs, shopped at the same stores, commuted on the same trains to the same offices. To newly arriving immigrants, clinging to the old language and culture was important; to succeeding generations, getting ahead in America mattered more. Thus, as the number of new immigrants dwindled, assimilation of ethnic minorities was inevitable. (The story of the earlier immigration is told in the volume in this series called *A Century of Immigration*.)

By the 1960s, the United States population no longer included many large immigrant minorities living in their own ethnic areas. Whereas in

1920 about 13 percent of the population was foreign born, in 1960 it was less than 6 percent. Congress now began to take another look at the immigration laws which had been passed in the early 1920s. These in general had been set up to reflect the ethnic complexion of the United States as it had been in 1890 or 1900 before the great burst of southern and eastern immigration of Italians, Poles, Jews, and others. Congress established quotas that for the English, Germans, and Irish were high, but for southern and eastern Europeans were low. There were no quotas for Asians. By the 1960s this seemed unfair. In 1965 Congress passed a law eliminating ethnic quotas; people would be admitted on a first-come, first-served basis. There would be a limit of 290,000 total each year.

In addition to the legal immigrants, there are many illegal entries. Here two Mexicans looking for work in the United States slip out of a grain hopper railroad car at Larado, Texas. They were quickly caught and sent back.

However, relatives of immigrants already in the United States would be allowed in outside the limit.

This, too, seemed only fair, and nobody gave it much thought. It was assumed that most immigrants would be Europeans, as they always had been. However, the people writing the new immigration law did not see that the world had changed. In the earlier time, especially in the 1800s, there had been much poverty, even famine, in places in Europe, especially Ireland, southern Italy, and Russia. By the 1960s Europe was growing prosperous. In addition, people from the Soviet Union and its captive nations, like Poland and Hungary, were not allowed to leave. Only relatively small numbers of Europeans could, or would want to, immigrate. On the other hand, by the 1960s people in much of Asia and Hispanic America were suffering from poverty and political oppression. There began a new wave of immigration by people mainly from Mexico, the Caribbean, Central America, India, Pakistan, Bangladesh, Korea, Vietnam, China, and other Asian and Hispanic nations.

Such people were eager to bring in their relatives. Thus an immigrant might bring in her brother, who would bring in his wife, who would bring in her mother, in a never-ending chain. Asian and Hispanic immigration rolls swelled. For example, in the 1940s there were about 17,000 Chinese immigrants; in the 1980s over 300,000. In the 1980s the Asian population of the United States grew seven times faster than the general population. By 1999, 12 percent of Americans were Hispanic; 2.7 percent were Asian born.

In the decade of the 1950s, for instance, about 1.5 million people arrived from Europe, along with fewer than half a million Hispanics. In the 1980s about 700,000 Europeans came and 2.5 million Hispanics. The growth of Asian immigration was even more striking. It increased from 157,000 in the 1950s to an estimated ten times that in the 1990s. Overall, the percent of the foreign-born in the total population began to increase from its low of 4.7 in 1970, so that by 2000 it was double that

This newsstand reflects the range of immigrants living in American cities. Immigrant groups often have their own newspapers and radio and television stations and speak their native languages among themselves.

at nearly 10 percent. A quarter of the foreign-born population was Mexican; 68.5 percent of the 25 million foreign-born in America in 2000 were Asian or Hispanic.

Attitudes toward the new immigrants were mixed. Right or wrong, people usually resent seeing a lot of newcomers speaking strange languages and following different customs move into their towns, their neighborhoods. This is as true of Africans and Asians as it is of Americans. Many Americans disliked the new wave of immigration and there was pressure to cut it back.

But there were others who favored expanded immigration, including of course the majority of immigrants themselves; and more significantly the agricultural, hotel, and other businesses that depended on them for cheap labor. Many people also believed that it was good for America for immigrants to hang onto their native cultures. Thus was born the idea that the United States was, or at least should be, a *multicultural* society where people of many different cultures, each clinging to their own folkways, could work together in harmony. There would not be an American culture as such, shared by all Americans; instead, each person would belong to whatever culture he or she chose. For the multiculturalist *diversity*, rather than *homogeneity* (meaning *consistency* or *uniformity*), was the goal.

Those who favored multiculturalism insisted that diversity brought America strength as well as variety of experience. Those opposed, like the distinguished historian Arthur Schlesinger, said that multiculturalism

The signs in New York City's Chinatown are in both Chinese and English. While immigrants usually continue to speak their own language at home, most must learn English and American ways to function in the larger society.

"reverses the historic theory of America as one people." People like Schlesinger feared that the nation, instead of sharing common bonds, would become a patchwork of competing ethnic groups.

However anyone felt about the argument, as a practical matter diversity could go only so far. Most immigrants found that in order to do their jobs and get ahead in business and the professions, they had at least to learn English. At home, of course, newcomers could speak their traditional languages, eat their traditional food, and generally follow the family customs of "the old country." Nevertheless, the new Hispanic and Asian immigrants would most likely see, as had all immigrant groups before them, their grandchildren grow up to adopt the lifestyle of mainstream America. This is particularly true of Asians, who tend to be better educated and have higher incomes than Americans of any ethnicity. They also marry non-Asians at a high rate.

A second demographic change that overtook the United States at the end of the twentieth century was the "aging" of the nation. The century saw a huge, indeed astonishing, number of improvements in medicine. Many new drugs, such as penicillin, were discovered and some of them almost overnight eliminated disease like tuberculosis that had been killing millions every year. Improved X-rays, CAT scans, and other tools allowed doctors to diagnose diseases much more accurately. The transplanting of organs like hearts and kidneys and the development of bypass operations allowed tens of thousands of people to live who would have died only a few decades before.

Nonetheless, many historians of medicine believe that more important than improved medical techniques were advances in sanitation and the general conditions of American life. Even into the twentieth century the water that millions drank was contaminated by sewage. Garbage-strewn streets and crowded slums spread disease. Improved sanitation of American cities, better methods of disposing of garbage, reduction of disease-bearing animals like rats, flies, and mosquitoes have kept people

Advances in medicine have allowed more children to grow up in good health and more people to live longer lives. Today older people often retire later, and frequently keep active with hobbies and volunteer work.

more healthy. There have been two results. One is that death in childhood has been markedly reduced. Even as recently as 1960, twenty-six of every thousand babies died as infants; by the turn of the century this figure had declined to just over seven of every thousand babies. This meant that in the year 2000 about 75,000 more children lived to grow up than would have in 1960.

Just as significantly, improved health has meant that Americans have been living longer. At the same time, they are having somewhat fewer children than they were having at an earlier time, particularly during the postwar baby boom. As a result, Americans are older than they used to be. The number of people over eighty-five doubled between 1970 and 1990; the number over a hundred doubled between 1980 and 1990. In 1950 about 8 percent of Americans were over sixty-five, by 2000 almost 12 percent were. As a consequence of all this, the nation is older: In

1900, 44 percent of the population were children and teenagers; in 2000 it had fallen to 29 percent. With many young couples delaying marriage and children; with many married couples living longer after their children left home; and many women having children alone, the idealized family of father, mother, and children made up fewer than 25 percent of households in 2000.

One important result of the aging of America (which also occurred in other industrial nations) is that more people lived many years after retirement. This in turn meant that Social Security benefits and pensions were taking a larger slice of the national pie, so that people still working had to give up more of their salaries in Social Security taxes and payments to pension plans than they had in the past. By the year 2000 the government was struggling to find ways to keep the Social Security system from running out of money.

One more significant demographic change of the second half of the twentieth century was a general movement from the northeastern part of the country to the South and West. Technology has driven this demographic movement, too. Air-conditioned buildings and cars allow people to live and work in the hot Southwest.

Taken as a whole, in the year 2000, the United States had changed from the nation it had been when World War II ended. The changes had brought with them problems. There was still friction over race relations and immigration. Many people felt that Americans had come to place too high a value on acquiring things—the most modern computer, a new car, the best entertainment system—in place of human values. Instead of talking over a cup of coffee with neighbors, enjoying a picnic with the family or a basketball game with friends, Americans were spending too much time staring at a television set or bent over the computer keyboard. People who thought about such things felt that in so doing many Americans were missing out on the most important part of life.

Yet despite the problems, Americans had much to be proud of. The nation was without question the most prosperous in the world and perhaps the most politically free as well. And that, really, has been the story, not only in this book but in the whole series called The Drama of American History. The nation will stay free only if its citizens understand its important institutions, how they worked, and how they developed over time. Knowing history matters, because it tells what sacrifices must be made and how much we must know in order to maintain our liberties.

BIBLIOGRAPHY

For Teachers

Branch, Taylor. *Parting the Waters: America in the King Years, 1954–1963*. New York: Simon & Schuster, 1988.

Burner, David. *Making Peace with the 60s*. Princeton, NJ: Princeton University Press, 1996.

Coontz, Stephanie. *The Way We Really Are: Coming to Terms with America's Changing Families*. New York: Basic Books, 1997.

Egan, Timothy. *Lasso the Wind: Away to the New West*. New York: Knopf/Distributed by Random House, 1998.

Gitlin, Todd. *The Sixties: Years of Hope, Days of Rage*. New York: Bantam Books, 1987.

Graham, Hugh Davis. *The Civil Rights Era: Origins and Development of National Policy, 1960–1972*. New York: Oxford University Press, 1989.

Halberstam, David. *The Fifties*. New York: Villard Books, 1993.

Hartman, Susan M. *From Margin to Mainstream: Women and American Politics Since 1960*. Philadelphia: Temple University Press, 1989.

Jackson, Kenneth T. *Crabgrass Frontier: the Suburbanization of the United States*. New York: Oxford University Press, 1985.

Lemann, Nicholas. *The Promised Land: The Great Black Migration and How It Changed America*. New York: Alfred A. Knopf, 1991.

Levy, Frank. *The New Dollars and Dreams: American Income in the Late 1990s*. New York: Russell Sage Foundation, 1998.

O'Neill, William. *American High: The Years of Confidence*. New York: The Free Press, 1986.

Reimers, David M. *Still the Golden Door: The Third World Comes to America*. 2nd ed. New York: Columbia University, 1992.

Schlesinger, Arthur M., Jr. *The Disuniting of America: Reflections on a Multicultural Society*. New York: W.W. Norton, 1992.

Sitkoff, Harvard. *The Struggle for Black Equality, 1954–1992*. New York: Hill and Wang, 1993.

Wolfe, Tom. *The Right Stuff*. New York: Farrar, Straus and Giroux, 1979.

For Students

Aldred, Lisa. *Thurgood Marshall: Supreme Court Justice*. New York: Chelsea House, 1990.

Brandon, Alexandra. *Mexican Americans*. New York: Silver Burdett, 1993.

Calabro, Marian. *Zap! A Brief History of Television*. New York: Four Winds, 1992.

Cole, Michael D. *John Glenn: Astronaut and Senator*. Springfield, NY: Enslow, 1993.

Curson, Marjorie N. *Jonas Salk*. Englewood Cliffs, NM: Silver Burdett, 1990.

Greenhaven Press, ed. *Culture Wars* (1999), *The Family* (1998),

Feminism (2001), *Immigration* (1998), *Sixties Counterculture* (2001). Westport, CT: Greenhaven Press.

Haskins, Jim. *I Have A Dream: The Life and Words of Martin Luther King, Jr.* Brookfield, CT: Millbrook Press, 1993.

Hendrickson, John. *Rachel Carson: The Environmental Movement.* Brookfield, CT: Millbrook Press, 1990.

Henry, Sondra, and Emily Taitz. *Betty Friedan: Fighter for Women's Rights.* Springfield, NJ: Enslow, 1990.

Lucas, Eileen. *Civil Rights: The Long Struggle.* Springfield, IL: Enslow, 1996.

Spangenberg, Ray, and Diane Moser. *History of Science from 1946 to the 1990s.* New York: Facts on File, 1994.

———. *Opening the Space Frontier: Space Exploration.* New York: Facts on File, 1989.

Takaki, Ronald. *Strangers at the Gates Again: Asian American Immigration After 1965.* New York: Farrar, Straus and Giroux, 1979.

Wolfe, Tom. *The Right Stuff.* New York: Farrar, Straus and Giroux, 1979.

Slavin, Ed. *Jimmy Carter.* New York: Chelsea House, 1989.

Sullivan, George. *George Bush.* New York: Julian Messner, 1989.

INDEX

JAMES LINCOLN COLLIER is the author of a number of books both for adults and for young people, including the social history *The Rise of Selfishness in America*. He is also noted for his biographies and historical studies in the field of jazz. Together with his brother, Christopher Collier, he has written a series of award-winning historical novels for children widely used in schools, including the Newbery Honor classic, *My Brother Sam Is Dead*. A graduate of Hamilton College, he lives with his wife in New York City.

CHRISTOPHER COLLIER grew up in Fairfield County, Connecticut and attended public schools there. He graduated from Clark University in Worcester, Massachusetts and earned M.A. and Ph.D. degrees at Columbia University in New York City. After service in the Army and teaching in secondary schools for several years, Mr. Collier began teaching college in 1961. He is now Professor of History at the University of Connecticut and Connecticut State Historian. Mr. Collier has published many scholarly and popular books and articles about Connecticut and American history. With his brother, James, he is the author of nine historical novels for young adults, the best known of which is *My Brother Sam Is Dead*. He lives with his wife Bonnie, a librarian, in Orange, Connecticut.